MEDITATION JOURNAL FOR TEENS

meditation JOURNAL for teens

GUIDED MEDITATIONS TO HELP YOU STAY COOL, CALM, AND PRESENT

SIMONE FINNIS, LMFT

ROCKRIDGE PRESS

For general information on our other products and services or to obtain technical support, please contact our Customer Care Department within the United States at (866) 744-2665, or outside the United States at (510) 253-0500.

Rockridge Press publishes its books in a variety of electronic and print formats. Some content that appears in print may not be available in electronic books, and vice versa.

TRADEMARKS: Rockridge Press and the Rockridge Press logo are trademarks or registered trademarks of Callisto Media Inc. and/or its affiliates, in the United States and other countries, and may not be used without written permission. All other trademarks are the property of their respective owners. Rockridge Press is not associated with any product or vendor mentioned in this book.

Interior and Cover Designer: Stephanie Mautone
Art Producer: Tom Hood
Editor: Eun H. Jeong
Production Editor: Mia Moran
Production Manager: Michael Kay

Cover and interior patterns courtesy of Photohacklovers/Creative Market
Author photograph courtesy of Thaymmie Cotto

ISBN: Print 978-1-64876-976-4
R0

THIS JOURNAL
BELONGS TO:

_____

CONTENTS

Your calm mind is the ultimate weapon against your challenges. so relax.

—Bryant McGill, *Simple Reminders: Inspiration for Living Your Best Life*

INTRODUCTION

Hello! Welcome to *Meditation Journal for Teens*. Whether you chose this book for yourself, came upon it by chance, or received it as a gift, I hope that you will find it a useful resource in your daily life.

You know as well as anyone, being a teen can be quite stressful. But your curiosity, your willingness to explore, and your commitment to applying some of what you learn from this journal can help you feel more relaxed and better able to cope with the challenges that may come your way.

Always keep in mind that you are fine just as you are—there is nothing "wrong" with you if you feel stressed or sad sometimes. We all feel that way at times. Still, all of us can benefit from learning new skills to help us be our best selves.

As a therapist who specializes in working with teens and their families, I have helped teens just like you reduce their anxiety, improve their grades, make better choices, develop more friendships, feel more connected to others, and feel happier and better about themselves.

I wrote this book to help you develop a sense of calm and well-being. My goal is also to help you handle the typical and some-times intense emotions and situations that you may face. Never meditated before? Don't worry. You can still use this book. Each medi-tation is explained step-by-step. You can try out different meditations and use the ones you feel most comfortable with. (See "How to Use This Journal" on page xiii for more information.)

Meditation has been practiced by many cultures for thousands of years. It can help you experience a greater feeling of peace by guiding you to relax your body, clear your mind, and increase your self-awareness. For some people, meditation is part of their spiritual practice. For others, it is simply part of their daily routine, like exercise. How you choose to use meditation in your life is up to you.

Meditation can take different forms. Some meditations are guided or silent, some focus on thoughtful movements like walking, and some focus on repeating a short phrase (a *mantra*) or a positive statement (an *affirmation*). There is even laughing meditation. In this book, you will get to try out several different kinds of meditations.

Practicing meditation can have many benefits, like better sleep, less muscle tension, less anxiety, and better mood. Some people notice that they focus better, and some even notice a greater sense of well-being. Meditating regularly can also help create a feeling of being "grounded." This means feeling calm and balanced even when you face challenges and concerns. Meditation can also help you be more aware of your thoughts and feelings. Your thoughts directly affect your feelings, which in turn influence your actions. For example, if you are thinking positive and optimistic thoughts, you most likely will feel upbeat and hopeful and do or say constructive things. Likewise, the opposite is true. The beauty of meditation is that it can not only help promote more awareness of your thoughts and feelings (mindfulness), but it can also support you in having more peaceful and serene thoughts and, therefore, more tranquil and relaxed feelings.

My wish for you is that no matter what you have experienced in the past or may be experiencing now, whether negative or positive, you will gain great benefits from using this journal.

HOW TO USE
THIS JOURNAL

This meditation journal is organized into four sections, each with an empowering and inspiring theme. Each section has 10 simple meditations followed by three journal prompts to help you reflect on your meditation experience as well as topics related to areas that many teens struggle with today.

Each meditation is intended to build on the one before. If you are new to meditation, I suggest you start with the first meditation of each section and proceed from there. Once you have done a few or if you already have some meditation experience, you can move around and choose specific sections or meditations that you feel may help you now.

You will get the greatest benefit if you set aside time daily or weekly to meditate and journal. If you cannot reflect on all three prompts, that is okay. Just do what you can, as long as you are consistent with practicing meditation. Like practicing a musical instrument or playing a sport, the practice of meditation becomes easier when it is done regularly. Journaling through the prompts will also help you keep track of your progress as you record your thoughts and feelings.

Keep in mind that this book is not a substitute for counseling. If you feel distress or any other negative emotions as you use this book, please reach out to an adult you trust or a mental health professional.

ONE

be here now

Maybe you have heard the saying "the present is a present." What does that mean? It means being able to stay in the present moment is a gift. And why is that? Because it stops you from dwelling on the past, which you have no control over anymore, and stops you from worrying about the future, which you have only limited control over.

When you are fully grounded in the present moment, you can feel free. This reduces stress and anxiety. This is helpful because feeling relaxed allows you to think more clearly and make better choices now, which can have a positive impact on your future. You will also be able to notice the small things that make life so wonderful, like someone's smile or your natural surroundings. Being present can also help you better understand and connect with your emotions, which will allow you to manage them in a healthier way.

I Am Focused on This Moment

1. Find a place to sit quietly.

2. Allow yourself to feel comfortable in this space with your back supported. Place your feet and hands in a comfortable position.

3. Take three slow, deep breaths, each one slower than the one before. Notice as your breath enters your nose and travels to your lungs.

4. Breathe naturally as you gently relax your eyelids.

5. Place one hand on your belly. Gently expand your belly with each breath.

6. Allow your entire body to relax as you continue this breathing for several minutes. Let any thoughts that come just float away like a cloud or boat as you continue to focus on your breath.

How did focusing on your breath allow you to stay in the present moment?

How do you think this practice might help you feel calmer?

What are the benefits of staying calm throughout your day?

I Am Calm in This Moment

1. Find a quiet spot to sit comfortably.

2. Close your eyes. Breathe in for four counts, hold for two counts, and then breathe out for six counts.

3. Repeat twice more. Let your body become more relaxed with each breath.

4. Picture a place or memory that makes you feel peaceful and happy.

5. Hold that picture for a few minutes. If it fades, that is okay. Allow it to come and go, but keep returning to it.

6. Focus on that feeling of peace and happiness.

7. Take two slow, deep breaths.

8. Gently open your eyes and focus again on your surroundings.

Describe in detail your happy place or memory.

_____

_____

_____

_____

_____

_____

_____

_____

_____

_____

What other feelings came up for you as you focused on this memory or picture? For example, did you feel confident, positive, or safe?

_____

_____

_____

_____

How do you think going back to this picture throughout your day might help you feel calm in any moment?

I Am Patient and Relaxed in This Moment

1. Sit in a comfortable position.

2. Breathe in and out gently.

3. Relax your eyelids.

4. Continue to breathe in and out gently.

5. Allow each area of your body to become soft and relaxed with each breath, starting from your head and going down to your toes. Do this for several minutes. Take your time. Don't rush yourself.

6. Quietly say to yourself:

   I am calm and patient in this moment.

   I am calm and patient with the people around me.

   I stay calm and patient in stressful situations.

7. Continue to breathe in and out gently.

8. Take this feeling of calm and patience with you as you go through your day.

It can be challenging to be patient in some situations. What are some of these situations for you?

How can being patient *in each moment* be more helpful than trying to think of being patient *all the time*?

Write in your journal about how it helped to take the feeling from your meditation through your day. Write down some of the benefits of patience. For example, were you able to finish your tasks faster? Did you feel less angry?

I Participate Fully
in My Day

1. Sit comfortably.

2. Notice all the sounds around you.

3. Allow those sounds to fade into the background as you focus on slowing your breath.

4. Turn your attention to your day ahead. Notice if your body tenses or stays the same. If you feel tension, slow your breath.

5. Try to imagine yourself breathing in a sense of calm and then breathing out your feeling of concern.

6. Imagine yourself focusing on and enjoying each activity in your day.

7. Picture yourself eager to participate in each activity while still calm and focused.

8. Breathe deeply and return your focus to your surroundings.

What was it like to allow the sounds to fade into the background? Was it easy or hard to do?

_____

_____

_____

_____

_____

_____

_____

_____

Do you sometimes just hurry through your activities or do them only half-heartedly? What was it like to imagine yourself focusing on each of your activities and enjoying them instead?

_____

_____

_____

_____

How would your day improve if you were able to stay calm and participate fully in all your activities?

I Listen and Focus on the Now

1. Take three deep breaths to clear your mind.

2. Listen carefully and focus on anyone who may be speaking to you.

3. Acknowledge them and reply calmly and clearly, if a reply is needed.

4. If your mind wanders, take three quiet, deep breaths and refocus.

5. Notice the words you hear.

6. Notice who is speaking.

7. Notice how they are speaking.

8. Notice how you are answering them.

9. Practice attentiveness as you continue throughout your day.

10. Congratulate yourself for your efforts.

How was it to listen attentively throughout your day? Was it helpful, stressful, or a bit of both? Why?

How can listening in a focused way help you stay grounded in the present moment?

What are some other benefits you found to listening carefully?

I Listen to Understand in This Moment

1. Begin by taking three deep, refreshing breaths.

2. Now try to remember a difficult conversation you had recently.

3. Close your eyes and try to see yourself taking part in this conversation.

4. Think about looking at and observing the person you were talking with.

5. Focus on what their body language was and what they were saying.

6. Focus on what your body language was and how you were listening.

7. Notice if you were listening to understand or just waiting for your turn to speak.

8. Notice if you completely understood what they were saying.

9. Breathe deeply and return your attention to your surroundings.

How did you notice yourself listening? Were you listening to understand or listening simply to make your own point? What do you think is the difference?

_____

_____

_____

_____

_____

_____

_____

Sometimes in a conversation we jump ahead and guess what someone is going to say instead of waiting and listening carefully to what they actually say. If you stayed more grounded in the present moment, do you think you would be able to listen better? Why or why not?

_____

_____

_____

_____

If you listen mindfully and carefully—in other words, give the other person your full attention—would that help you stay more in the present moment? How could this practice help you better connect with others?

I Eat Intentionally

1. Find something to eat. It can be a piece of fruit or a vegetable, like an apple or carrot.

2. As you prepare to eat, take three slow, deep breaths.

3. With each exhale, clear away any distractions or concerns from your mind.

4. With each inhale, focus on your food.

5. Observe your food's smell and how it looks without judging.

6. Think about who grew the food and all the effort it took for it to be in your hand right now.

7. Take your first bite. Notice how it feels as you chew.

8. Allow yourself to enjoy the taste and smell of your food.

9. Think thoughts of appreciation for the food's nourishment and for the people who produced it.

10. Practice these steps with each meal.

Do you tend to eat mindfully (with attention to your food) or in a distracted way?

Describe what it was like to eat thoughtfully and intentionally.

How can this practice help you when you eat a meal?
Does being more present with your meal make it a more
enjoyable or pleasant experience? If yes, how?

I Focus on What Is Mine to Do in This Moment

VISUALIZATION MEDITATION

1. Sit or lie down somewhere comfortable.

2. Remain alert by focusing on breathing in gently through your nose and out through your mouth.

3. Continue this breathing until you are completely relaxed but still alert.

4. Gently focus on each distraction around you and then picture each one disappearing, like a puff of smoke or a balloon floating away.

5. Continue to breathe gently.

6. Now picture typical distractions that interfere with your day, like videos, social media, TV, and talking.

7. Imagine their pull on your attention disappearing as you complete your daily tasks, like homework or chores.

8. Breathe deeply as you let your mind focus on what you need to do and ignore all distractions.

Have you ever noticed yourself getting distracted during the day? What are some of your main distractions?

_____

_____

_____

_____

_____

_____

_____

_____

_____

Sometimes it is easy or even enjoyable to get distracted. How was it to imagine the pull of distractions having less power over you? Was it scary, or did you feel freer?

_____

_____

_____

_____

What would your day be like if you were able to focus on and finish what you had to do in each moment?

I Move Intentionally

MOVEMENT MEDITATION

1. As you prepare for your day or your evening, take three deep, refreshing breaths.

2. Allow each breath to make you feel relaxed and ready for whatever comes next in your day or evening.

3. Stand up and walk around the room, if you are able. With each step, notice your posture.

4. Notice as you place each foot in front of the other or notice how you move about if you are unable to use your legs.

5. Notice the force on your legs and feet or other parts of your body as you proceed.

6. Notice a feeling of being grounded as you connect with each movement.

7. Practice doing this meditation each day.

What was it like to mindfully notice your movements? Was it difficult or easy? Do you think you can apply this meditation to other parts of your body?

Did you find that you made judgments about your movements or yourself as you moved about? If so, why? Can you let any judgments go?

Do you think moving with intention through your day can help you stay more in the present? Why or why not?

I Am Fully in
This Moment

FOCUSED MEDITATION

1. Find a small object to hold that brings you joy.

2. Comfortably adjust your body in a seated or lying down position.

3. Breathe slowly and gently, in and out.

4. Now focus on the object, holding it gently in your hand. Notice how it feels when touched. Describe it in your mind. Is it soft, smooth, rough, textured?

5. Notice how it is shaped and if it has a smell.

6. Notice if it makes a sound when squeezed gently.

7. Continue to observe the item while breathing.

8. Return to the present moment.

What was the feeling or reaction you had from holding and observing the object? For example, did it give you a feeling of comfort or make you smile? Describe your experience.

_____

_____

_____

_____

_____

_____

_____

How was it to use four of your five senses to intentionally observe this item? Could this practice help you feel grounded in the present moment? How?

_____

_____

_____

**Can you use your senses during your day to become
more present? Explain.**

this is me

A re you sometimes influenced or negatively affected by what others think of you? Do you ever find yourself wishing you were someone else? Maybe you do not think you have something valuable to contribute to your friend group, family, or community. Hiding yourself or not valuing who you are can be destructive to your self-confidence and self-esteem. It can also prevent you from sharing your unique ideas, gifts, and talents with the world.

This section focuses on recognizing your value and increasing your self-worth. Feeling valued is not always easy because we frequently receive unsupportive messages from the media and sometimes even from friends and family members. But with practice and determination, you can learn to be true to who you are, feel more confident, and express yourself in a more positive way.

These meditations are focused on your own inner messages and beliefs; they are not about changing how others think of you. *If at any time you feel that expressing yourself might not be supported by others or might place you in an uncomfortable situation, please reach out to a trusted adult or mental health professional.*

I Accept Myself

1. Find a comfortable sitting position.

2. Breathe gently for a few minutes with your eyes closed fully or partially.

3. Imagine wrapping yourself in a warm, cozy blanket that represents love and acceptance.

4. Allow yourself to feel love all around you. Allow yourself to feel acceptance of all of you.

5. Repeat gently to yourself:

   I am okay just the way I am.

   I am free to be me.

   I am enough.

6. Take a deep breath.

7. Repeat these positive statements (affirmations) to yourself once more, slowly.

8. Imagine yourself going through your day with that warm blanket of love and self-acceptance wrapped around you.

What was it like to focus on these affirmations about yourself? Was it difficult or easy? Why?

How did the blanket metaphor work for you? What other metaphor could you use that would help you feel self-love?

Why do you think it is important to practice self-acceptance?

I Am Unique

1. Lie or sit comfortably.

2. Slow your breathing while noticing your breath on each inhale and exhale.

3. Close your eyes if that is comfortable for you.

4. Think about two or three characteristics or traits that you like about yourself.

5. If you notice any negative thoughts creeping in, gently bring your focus back to your list.

6. Acknowledge these characteristics or traits as things that make you unique. Smile as you think of each characteristic or trait.

7. Know and repeat silently to yourself: "There is only one me, and no one can replace me."

8. Continue to meditate on these ideas as you breathe gently and slowly.

9. Allow yourself to accept that you are special in your own unique way.

How was it to focus on what you appreciate about yourself instead of criticizing yourself?

Have you ever thought of yourself and how you express yourself as being unique? Why or why not?

How is focusing on these qualities less likely to make you compare yourself to others? What might happen for you if you compared yourself to others less?

I Expand My Voice

1. Take three deep, powerful breaths.

2. Repeat each of the following affirmations, and after each one, take a deep breath:

   My voice matters.

   My opinion matters.

   I matter.

   I can and I will share who I am through what I say and how I say it.

   I know what to say in conversations and am mindful of the best time to say it.

   When I express myself, I can help others express themselves, too.

3. Repeat these statements as many times as you like, allowing yourself to feel stronger each time.

4. Finish by taking three more deep, powerful breaths.

Do you sometimes find you can't express yourself in certain situations? Describe when this happens.

_____

_____

_____

_____

_____

_____

_____

What gets in your way of expressing yourself? What would you like to be different?

_____

_____

_____

_____

_____

How can it be helpful to remind yourself of these affirmations in your daily life?

I Allow Myself to Be Imperfect

1. Focus on your breath as you breathe in gently for a few moments.

2. Now think of a time when you made a mistake or felt embarrassed by your actions or your appearance.

3. Continue to breathe attentively, noticing any emotions that come up and letting them float away.

4. Imagine writing down a description of your mistake or embarrassment on a piece of paper, but give the main character of this story a different name.

5. Imagine yourself comforting that person. Let them know you understand how they feel and that it's okay.

6. Now turn those comforting feelings toward yourself.

7. Think back to that piece of paper and imagine crumpling it up and throwing it away, along with any feelings of shame or self-judgment.

8. Breathe deeply as you continue to send feelings of comfort and compassion toward yourself.

Are there times you expect yourself to be perfect, either in your looks or in your actions? Name a few of these times. Are you willing to let this expectation of perfection go?

_____

_____

_____

_____

_____

_____

_____

_____

Sometimes we believe that striving for perfection makes us work harder or that others will like us more if they see us as perfect. Have you ever thought this? Explain.

_____

_____

_____

How is this type of thinking unhelpful? What can you think instead that would be more helpful?

I Trust Myself

1. Breathe deeply and allow your body to relax.

2. Notice how your breath flows naturally or how your heart beats naturally on its own.

3. Focus on how your body knows how to do these functions on its own.

4. Think about how you trust your body to do these things.

5. Consider what it would be like to trust yourself in this way. Do you feel more confident?

6. Allow yourself to believe in your instincts, thoughts, and decisions.

7. Notice what it feels like to trust freely instead of having self-doubt.

8. Continue to breathe deeply as you let that feeling fill your body.

What are some other things you trust your body to do? For example, you likely trust your body to tell you when you are hungry. What else?

How would having less self-doubt change how you interact with others?

If you find that you regularly doubt your thoughts, feelings, and actions, what goal could you have to change this? What things could you do to help you achieve this goal?

I Discover My Passions

1. Settle into a comfortable position.

2. Allow your breath to calm and relax you. Close your eyes if that is comfortable for you.

3. Imagine yourself in a garden with various small rocks. Written under each rock is a description of something you care deeply about. Is it music? Your friends? What do you want to be in the future?

4. Picture yourself looking under each rock and choosing the ones that inspire or motivate you the most.

5. Breathe deeply as you return your awareness to your surroundings.

Our passions are connected to things we care deeply about. What descriptions did you see, or what sense did you get about what your passions are?

_____

_____

_____

_____

_____

_____

_____

_____

What are two things you realize you care most deeply about? For example, do you care about helping others, the planet, animals, or becoming a professional athlete or scientist?

_____

_____

_____

What did you learn about yourself and what you are passionate about from doing this meditation?

I Follow My Dreams

1. Find a quiet space.

2. Breathe in and out softly and steadily. Let your body relax.

3. Begin to imagine your most important dream, the one you wish for the most.

4. Paint a picture of this dream in your mind. What does it look like? What are you doing?

5. See yourself moving toward that dream.

6. Notice the feelings you have as you get closer to your dream.

7. Repeat this meditation for other dreams you may have.

How was it to visualize getting closer to your dream? Did it cause worry, excitement, or something else? Explain.

What are some of the habits you think you need to have or develop to pursue your dream?

While it is important to realize that others will not always see your dreams as you see them, it can still be helpful to seek support. To whom could you turn for this support?

I Value My Talents

1. Take a moment to calm your mind by taking a few deep breaths.

2. As you become more relaxed, start to think about your strengths or talents. These may be big or small, come naturally to you, or be ones you developed over time.

3. Compliment yourself to show appreciation for your strengths or talents. Avoid judging yourself.

4. Repeat quietly to yourself:

   My talents are unique to me.

   I cherish my talents.

   I make use of my talents in a positive way.

5. Return to this meditation often to remind yourself of your unique strengths and talents.

Do you think it is important to use your talents for the good of others and not just yourself? Why or why not?

_____

_____

_____

_____

_____

_____

_____

_____

What do you think it means to cherish your talents?

_____

_____

_____

_____

_____

A talent can be natural (a great singing voice) or something you have developed over time (how to play the guitar). List some of your talents as you see them.

I Am Free to Be Me

1. Take three deep breaths to settle your mind and clear your thoughts.

2. Place one hand on your heart if that is comfortable for you.

3. With each breath, allow your heart to feel open. Picture a door in your heart opening if that is helpful.

4. Take another three breaths.

5. Now allow your mind to feel open.

6. With an open mind and heart, imagine what it feels like to be free to be yourself.

7. Take another deep breath. Notice any emotions that may come up and let them go.

8. Continue to breathe deeply as you see yourself being true to you.

9. Remove your hand from your heart, if you placed it there.

10. Return your attention to your surroundings.

Some people think being free means doing what they want, when they want. What do you think this meditation is referring to instead?

Being true to yourself is sometimes referred to as being *authentic*. Do you find that you are not authentic sometimes? Why is that?

What feelings came up for you as you imagined yourself being free to be you? Describe them.

I Accept My Body

1. Sit quietly and turn your attention to your breath.

2. Breathe gently and slowly.

3. Create a picture of yourself as you continue to breathe. Avoid judging any part of yourself.

4. Imagine giving yourself a warm hug, like you would hug a baby or your best friend. If it is comfortable for you, wrap your arms around yourself.

5. Starting from your head and moving down to your toes, send gentle, loving, and thankful thoughts to each and every part of you.

Do you sometimes compare yourself physically to others? If so, why? What are some loving thoughts you can send to your body?

_____

_____

_____

_____

_____

_____

_____

_____

Think about a band with all the different instruments and musicians and the beautiful music they create together. Now think about your body with all its different parts and functions and how it supports you throughout your whole day. How does having this thought make you feel?

_____

_____

_____

**How do you think you would feel if you fully accepted
your body as it is without comparing it to anyone else's?**

THREE

move past the struggle

When things get difficult—at home or at school, with parents or with friends—it's natural to feel emotions such as anxiety, fear, jealousy, and anger. At other times, you may feel those emotions just by picking them up from the people around you, or you may not know why you are feeling the way you do. Sometimes it can seem like these emotions are exploding inside you and you have no control over them. You may end up expressing these emotions in a negative way, which can lead to a worse situation.

Although you can't control every difficult situation, you can learn how to manage your emotions, thoughts, and actions so you can express yourself in a healthier and more positive way. Learning and practicing how to manage your emotions will help you see things more clearly and feel more peaceful and less stressed. *However, if you have negative emotions that do not seem to go away, please seek help from a trusted adult or mental health professional.*

I Am Confident
My Challenges Will
Work Out

1. Sit comfortably in an area without distractions.

2. Breathe gently and slowly. Allow your body and mind to slowly relax.

3. Bring to your mind one situation that challenges you. Observe it without judging it or anyone involved.

4. Take a deep breath and consciously release the worry and concern you have about this challenge.

5. Repeat three deep breaths.

6. Imagine your breath as a broom sweeping away the problem.

7. Now think of a time when you have been able to solve a problem. Was it a math problem? Was it stopping friends from fighting? Recall any ideas or skills you used or others who helped.

8. Reassure yourself that this problem, too, will be resolved.

How was it to sweep the problem away? Explain.

_____

_____

_____

_____

_____

_____

_____

_____

What helpful ideas came up for you?

_____

_____

_____

_____

_____

How can you continue to reassure yourself until the problem works out?

I Identify My Feelings

1. Find a quiet spot where you can sit or lie down comfortably.

2. Turn your attention to your breath and begin to breathe slowly and deeply.

3. After a few moments, focus on identifying a feeling you have in this moment. Are you feeling relaxed, annoyed, angry, happy, or upset? Are you feeling neutral?

4. Observe your feeling in detail.

5. Notice how the feeling is affecting your body. Continue the slow breaths.

6. Now choose an animal that could represent that feeling.

7. Identify what qualities this animal has that represent the feeling.

8. Breathe deeply.

9. Return your attention to your surroundings.

Was it easy or hard to identify a feeling? How come?

_____

_____

_____

_____

_____

_____

_____

_____

_____

_____

If identifying a feeling and connecting to it was a challenge, what would make it easier for you?

_____

_____

_____

_____

What animal did you choose to represent your feeling? What made you choose that animal?

I Let Go of Anger

1. Turn your attention to your breath.

2. Inhale and expand your stomach. Hold, and then release the breath, pushing all the air out and letting your stomach deflate.

3. Repeat once more.

4. Now, breathing slowly, picture a time when you were angry and showed your anger in a forceful way.

5. Picture those anger emotions as trapped in a balloon that is inflating, getting bigger and bigger.

6. Breathe in again, expanding your stomach.

7. Now quickly exhale all the air, deflating your stomach. As you breathe out, imagine the balloon releasing the anger emotions.

8. Repeat this once more: Breathe in, and then release all the air along with the anger emotions.

9. Continue to breathe slowly and gently as you return to your surroundings.

Do you sometimes show your anger emotions in a forceful or uncontrollable way? When are those times? How would you like to show those emotions instead?

How helpful was it to imagine the balloon releasing the anger emotions? Describe the experience. What other healthy ways can you imagine releasing intense anger emotions?

Can anger emotions be *constructive* rather than *destructive*? For example, if you see someone being bullied and you get upset enough to go to find help, that's constructive. Punching a wall if you get angry is destructive. List some of the ways anger can be constructive.

I Express My Feelings and Emotions Clearly and Appropriately

1. Sit or lie down comfortably.

2. Begin to breathe gently in and out.

3. Think about the range of feelings and emotions you have throughout a day.

4. Picture those emotions as playing out in a movie called *How I Express My Feelings*.

5. Notice the range of those emotions—for instance, intense or mild, negative or positive.

6. Continue to watch the movie to see how you express those emotions. Do you hold back your emotions or let them out in an uncontrollable way?

7. Keep watching the movie to see what happens after you express each emotion.

8. Now become the director and create scenes where you express your feelings clearly, calmly, and respectfully.

9. Continue to breathe gently as you return your attention to your surroundings.

What did you notice as you were watching the movie
How I Express My Feelings? **What would you change?**
What would you keep the same?

Some of us express our negative feelings in an angry,
sarcastic, or blaming way. Have you ever done that?
When were those times? What was the result?

What does it mean to "share your feelings in a healthy way"? How can you practice doing this?

I Accept Failure Graciously

1. Take a deep breath as you focus on relaxing your body.

2. Keep your attention on your breath as you slowly inhale and exhale.

3. Now turn your thoughts to a time when you felt you failed. Recall this memory without dwelling on the event.

4. Take a moment to consider the reactions you had to the event. Were you judging yourself harshly? Were you concerned about what others thought of you?

5. Breathe deeply.

6. With your inhale, choose to see failure as an opportunity to grow and learn.

7. With your exhale, release any negative opinions you have about yourself and failure.

8. Repeat quietly to yourself:

   Failure does not define me. I define me.

   I get a chance to discover and develop in new ways.

   I do my best with what I know.

   I still appreciate me.

Are there times when you believed you had failed at something and had a hard time dealing with that? Describe your experience.

_____

_____

_____

_____

_____

_____

_____

_____

What are some benefits to recognizing your failures? For example, perhaps you will learn a new way of doing things when you try again.

_____

_____

_____

_____

How can accepting and letting go of negative feelings, like disappointment or shame about failure, be helpful to you?

I Calm My Mind and Body

1. Find a comfortable seated or standing position.

2. Take a slow, deep breath and allow your mind to relax.

3. Take another slow, deep breath and allow your body to relax.

4. Repeat steps 2 and 3.

5. Take another deep breath; then exhale through your mouth as a sigh and let your shoulders drop.

6. Take another deep breath; then exhale through your mouth as a sigh and let your stomach go.

7. Now place or imagine a hand on your heart. Breathe in deeply and slowly three times.

8. Allow your heartbeat to slow down with each breath.

9. Slowly return your focus to your surroundings.

At times you may feel anxious or fearful. What are some of those times for you?

_____

_____

_____

_____

_____

_____

_____

_____

How can breathing purposefully, as in this meditation, help you feel calmer and more relaxed?

_____

_____

_____

_____

_____

What are some other ways you can help yourself relax or stay calm during stressful situations?

I Don't Give Up

1. Turn your focus to your breath.

2. Notice your breath as you inhale and exhale.

3. Shift your focus to your body. Notice as it relaxes with each breath.

4. Now imagine yourself as an ant. Picture the ant as it scurries along and continues its journey even when an obstacle is placed in its path.

5. Now imagine yourself as a tortoise. Picture the tortoise as it makes slow and steady progress toward its destination.

6. Continue to use your imagination to watch these creatures as they move with purpose.

7. Breathe deeply and return your attention to the present moment.

What can you learn from the ant and the tortoise? Explain.

How is the ant small yet mighty? How is the tortoise slow yet successful?

Perseverance means to stick with something and not give up. Can you recall times when you persevered? Would remembering these times help you when you are faced with a tough situation? How?

I Allow Myself to Feel Comforted

1. Find a place to sit or stand comfortably.

2. Rub your hands together and feel the warmth the rubbing creates. If easier, you can imagine doing this step instead.

3. Place or imagine your hands on your heart.

4. Breathe deeply and slowly. Feel your chest rise and fall with each breath.

5. Picture the warmth of your hands flowing into your heart and then spreading through your entire body.

6. Rub your hands together and place them on your heart again. If easier, you can imagine doing this step instead.

7. Now send the warmth of your hands to any place in your body where you feel sadness or upset.

8. Imagine that warm sensation is a kind energy soothing the unhappy feelings. Let yourself accept any feelings of comfort you may feel.

9. Continue to breathe deeply (through the feelings).

10. Practice these steps anytime you need to feel a sense of comfort.

Many young people have feelings of upset or unhappiness. Are there times when you feel sad or upset? Explain.

_____

_____

_____

_____

_____

_____

_____

_____

_____

How was it helpful to allow yourself to feel comforted in this moment? What other healthy methods have you found helpful to deal with unhappy feelings?

_____

_____

_____

_____

It can be helpful to turn to people you trust when you are experiencing difficult emotions. To whom do you turn, and how have they comforted you? (See page 131 for additional resources you can turn to for support.)

I Have a Good Attitude

1. Sit or lie down comfortably while remaining alert.

2. Take three deep, cleansing breaths. Close your eyes if that is comfortable for you.

3. Think of a difficult situation you have experienced recently.

4. Breathe deeply again, but slowly this time.

5. Without judgment, consider how you approached this situation. Were you constructive or critical? Were you negative, positive, or neutral?

6. Breathe deeply.

7. Picture your attitude and thoughts as clouds. See the negative and critical ones drifting away, leaving the positive and helpful ones behind.

8. Breathe deeply again, shifting your focus to the positive, constructive, and neutral clouds.

9. Return your attention to your surroundings.

If you were to draw clouds, what words would you fill in to describe your negative and critical clouds? What words would you fill in to describe your positive, constructive, and neutral clouds?

What does it mean to have a good attitude? Why is it helpful to have a good attitude, especially in stressful situations?

How can you practice having a good attitude each day?

I Am Gentle with Myself

1. Find a quiet spot where you can sit or stand comfortably.

2. Turn your attention to your breath as you slowly inhale and exhale.

3. Breathe in calm and breathe out any tension in your body.

4. Imagine your breath as a gentle wave entering and leaving your body.

5. Let your body relax even more.

6. Think about your gentle breath like how you can treat yourself. Think about how your breath doesn't judge you or get frustrated with you. Instead, it is always supporting you.

7. With each breath:

   Breathe in loving-kindness for yourself and breathe out disapproval.

   Breathe in appreciation and breathe out guilt.

   Breathe in compassion and breathe out embarrassment.

8. Return your attention to your surroundings and keep the feelings you breathed in with you.

What do you think it means to be gentle with yourself?

_____

_____

_____

_____

_____

_____

_____

_____

_____

_____

How can this gentleness with yourself help you when you are worried or stressed?

_____

_____

_____

_____

List some other ways you can care for yourself.

attitude of gratitude

What does an attitude of gratitude mean? It means choosing, with intention, to be thankful when things are good *and* when they are not. It means taking the time and making the effort to develop and express appreciation for your life, the people around you, and even the things in your life that help you function.

Please note that you are not expected to be grateful when bad things happen to you or others treat you poorly. However, you *can* appreciate your strength and resilience and be grateful to others who help you in tough times.

An attitude of gratitude not only helps you feel deep joy, but it also helps you feel a deeper connection to yourself and others. It can also help you cope better. Developing an attitude of gratitude can be your superpower, making you stronger when times are especially challenging.

In this section, it is important not to judge yourself for either not practicing appreciation or not practicing it as much as you would like. Use these meditations to become more aware of for whom and what you can be grateful. Learning something new takes time and energy. It is a journey, not a destination.

I Am Thankful for Little Things

1. Take a breath and gently close your eyes.

2. Imagine going through your day or evening.

3. Carefully notice the small things that you get done, whether you do them on your own or someone helps you.

4. Notice brushing your teeth. Notice getting dressed. Notice drinking or eating a meal.

5. As you picture each activity, express gratitude by completing this statement:

   I am thankful that I was able to _____.

6. Continue to imagine a few other small things you can appreciate.

7. Take a deep breath and return to your surroundings.

What did you notice about yourself as you intentionally appreciated the little things that you may take for granted?

_____

_____

_____

_____

_____

_____

_____

_____

_____

What were some of the small things you pictured that you could appreciate?

_____

_____

_____

_____

What would happen if you practiced noticing small things to appreciate in all parts of your daily life?

I Am Grateful for Life

1. Sit or lie down comfortably.

2. Take a deep, gentle breath and slowly lower your eyelids.

3. Repeat your gentle breath, fully closing your eyes if that is comfortable for you.

4. Focus on your gentle, steady breathing.

5. Listen to your breath as you inhale and exhale. Feel yourself relax.

6. Think about all the areas of your life that have been interesting, inspiring, exciting, and valuable to you. Now consider parts of your life that are boring, routine, uninspiring, and challenging.

7. Continue to breathe gently.

8. Consider that the good and the not-so-good parts of your life mean that you are fully alive to have different experiences.

9. Take a deep breath and return to your surroundings.

**What are some of the things you were able to
picture that were interesting, inspiring, exciting,
or valuable to you?**

_____

_____

_____

_____

_____

_____

_____

_____

_____

_____

**Sometimes it is easier to focus on things that are boring,
disappointing, or hard. How was it to recognize and be
thankful for the different types of experiences you have
in your life?**

_____

_____

_____

_____

What parts of your life contribute to your happiness? What parts contribute to your growth as a person? What parts have helped you learn more about yourself?

I Spread Peace
in My World

1. Take a few moments to breathe in deeply and slowly.

2. Center yourself in your breath.

3. Notice the sensations in your body as you inhale and exhale.

4. Continue this breathing for a few minutes.

5. Allow your body to relax and your mind to become peaceful. Let any thoughts that arise drift away.

6. Now imagine a feeling of calm washing over you like a warm shower.

7. Allow that feeling to sink into your entire being as you relax even more.

8. Imagine yourself taking that feeling of peace with you into your world.

When do you feel most peaceful?

How else can you create peaceful feelings in your life?

Why is it important to share and encourage peace with others?

I Am Full of Joy

1. Find a comfortable position sitting or lying down.

2. Take three deep, cleansing breaths. Allow your body to relax after each breath.

3. Now picture your heart as having a door.

4. Open this door, and imagine letting out any tension, stress, or worry held there.

5. Imagine that as these negative feelings leave, you come to a place in your heart where optimism, cheerfulness, and delight live.

6. Breathe deeply, focusing on these feelings. Allow them to grow.

7. Imagine opening the door to your heart even wider. See these joyful feelings spilling out into your surroundings.

8. Allow these feelings to fill you and surround you.

How did it feel to picture opening your heart and releasing negative feelings?

Often happiness is equated with joyfulness. But they are actually different. Happiness is sometimes temporary, and it tends to change depending on what is happening in your life. Joyfulness is more of a permanent quality, and it is about contentment in all situations. Which would you prefer to experience more of in your life, and why?

How was it to picture joy as coming from deep inside
your heart versus coming from something outside you?

I Appreciate My Body

1. Find a quiet place to sit or lie down comfortably.

2. Breathe in a gentle breath and hold for four counts; then release.

3. Repeat once more.

4. Gently wrap or imagine your arms around yourself and smile in appreciation of your body.

5. Place or imagine placing your hand on your head and smile in appreciation of your head. Breathe.

6. Place or imagine placing your hands on your shoulders and smile in appreciation of your shoulders. Breathe.

7. Place or imagine placing your hands on your stomach and smile in appreciation of your stomach. Breathe.

8. Repeat this with other parts of your body that you choose.

9. Continue to breathe as you consider how your body supports you.

What other parts of your body did you choose to appreciate? Why did you choose these parts?

_____

_____

_____

_____

_____

_____

_____

_____

_____

Why do you think it is important to appreciate your body?

_____

_____

_____

_____

How did it feel to smile in appreciation of different parts of your body?

I Am Thankful for Others

1. Sit or lie down comfortably.

2. Inhale and exhale quickly. Repeat.

3. Now slow your breath and focus on inhaling and exhaling deeply.

4. Imagine looking at photographs of people you care about.

5. Send each person a thought of gratitude and appreciation.

6. Repeat quietly to yourself:

   I appreciate you.

   Thank you for being in my life.

7. Now picture other people who play an important role in your life—for example, a helpful teacher or coach.

8. Send these people thoughts of gratitude and appreciation as well.

9. Return your attention to your surroundings.

Are there times when you take other people for granted? What are some ways you can show your appreciation of them?

How was it to send thoughts of appreciation and gratitude not only to those you care about but to others in your life as well?

Can appreciating other people help us feel more connected to them? How?

I Easily Express My Gratitude

1. Going about your day or evening, turn your attention to your breath.

2. Inhale and exhale slowly.

3. Notice any action someone does that you can be thankful for.

4. Take a deep, strong breath.

5. Now give a wholehearted thank-you to this person.

6. Tell them what you are thankful for and how it affected you.

7. Notice your feelings as you thoughtfully and enthusiastically express gratitude to another person.

Have you ever found it hard to say thank you to another person or express gratitude to them? If yes, what made it difficult?

How was it to express your gratitude in a complete way instead of only saying "thank you"? How do you think your life would change if you followed this practice regularly?

What feelings did you notice in yourself as you expressed thankfulness? Do you think expressions of gratitude benefit others, benefit yourself, or both? Explain.

I Value Our Differences

1. Take a deep, gentle breath and allow your body to relax.

2. Take another deep, gentle breath and allow your mind to relax.

3. Take a moment to think about people in your life who you consider to be different from you in some way and who would consider you to be different from them.

4. Consider the ways you think they are different. Is it beliefs, skin color, the way they dress, or something else?

5. Breathe gently in and gently out.

6. Now, with purpose and intention, choose to respect all the differences you noted.

7. Allow yourself to see the value of others even if they are different from you.

Do you think as humans we are more alike than we are different? Why or why not? What are some ways that we are all alike?

_____

_____

_____

_____

_____

_____

_____

_____

How important is it for you to feel respected and valued? Was it challenging for you to feel respect for others you see as different? Explain.

_____

_____

_____

_____

What can you learn from others who are different from you? What are some ways you can show others you value them?

I Care about My World

1. Sit or lie down comfortably.

2. Inhale slowly through your nose and exhale gently through your mouth.

3. Allow your body and mind to relax with each gentle breath.

4. Imagine looking at Earth as if you were viewing the planet from space. Notice the oceans, the land, and the North and South Poles.

5. Now imagine yourself closer to Earth—maybe in a plane as you fly over cities and towns and see homes and communities. Notice parks, lakes, farms, hills, and buildings.

6. Zoom in closer and imagine yourself in your own community. Notice the people around you, animals, your friends, and your loved ones.

7. Breathe deeply as you send loving, caring thoughts to the planet, your world, and your community.

What was it like to picture the planet Earth in this way? What were some of the loving, caring thoughts you sent to your world and your community?

_____

_____

_____

_____

_____

_____

_____

_____

_____

Do you think it is important to care about your world or your community? Why or why not?

_____

_____

_____

_____

What are some practical things you can do to care for the planet or your immediate neighborhood?

Loving-Kindness Meditation

1. Find a quiet area to sit or lie down comfortably.

2. Breathe in and out softly. Gently close your eyes if that is comfortable for you.

3. Become mindful of your body; notice how it feels in this moment.

4. Notice your breath as it enters and leaves your body.

5. Feel your body becoming more and more relaxed as you continue to breathe softly.

6. Now imagine the sun's rays beaming down on you.

7. Feel the warm, beautiful rays of light as beams of love and compassion surrounding you.

8. Let these feelings flow into your heart and through your entire body.

9. Allow yourself to accept these feelings of love, kindness, and compassion.

10. Continue to breathe softly as you gently return to your surroundings.

What did you notice about yourself as you accepted feelings of love, kindness, and compassion? Was it difficult or easy?

_____

_____

_____

_____

_____

_____

_____

_____

_____

Why do you think it is important to direct loving-kindness to yourself?

_____

_____

_____

_____

_____

How would your life be different if you intentionally practiced loving yourself and being compassionate with yourself?

> *Meditation is the ultimate mobile device; you can use it anywhere, anytime, unobtrusively.*

—Sharon Salzberg, *Real Happiness: A 28-Day Program to Realize the Power of Meditation*

RESOURCES

Books

Bluth, Karen. *The Self-Compassionate Teen: Mindfulness and Compassion Skills to Conquer Your Critical Inner Voice.* Oakland, CA: New Harbinger Publications, 2020.

Biegel, Gina. *Take In the Good: Skills for Staying Positive and Living Your Best Life.* Boulder, CO: Shambhala Publications, 2020.

Cain, Susan, Gregory Mone, and Erica Moroz. *Quiet Power: The Secret Strengths of Introverted Kids.* New York: Dial Books, 2016.

Halloran, Janine. *Coping Skills for Teens Workbook: 60 Helpful Ways to Deal with Stress, Anxiety and Anger.* Braintree, MA: Encourage Play, LLC, 2020.

Hannay, Catharine. *Being You: A Girl's Guide to Mindfulness.* Waco, TX: Prufrock Press, Inc., 2019.

Hansen, Mark Victor, Kimberly Kirberger, and Jack Canfield. *Chicken Soup for the Teenage Soul: 101 Stories of Life, Love and Learning.* Deerfield Beach, FL: Health Communications, Inc., 1997.

Hutt, Rachel. *Feeling Better: CBT Workbook for Teens: Essential Skills and Activities to Help You Manage Moods, Boost Self-Esteem, and Conquer Anxiety.* Emeryville, CA: Althea Press, 2019.

Kissen, Debra, Micah Ioffe, Michelle Lozano, and Ashley D. Kendall. *Rewire Your Anxious Brain for Teens: Using CBT, Neuroscience, and Mindfulness to Help You End Anxiety, Panic, and Worry.* Oakland, CA: New Harbinger Publications, 2020.

Van Dijk, Sheri. *Don't Let Your Emotions Run Your Life for Teens: Dialectical Behavior Therapy Skills for Helping You Manage Mood Swings, Control Angry Outbursts, and Get Along with Others.* Oakland, CA: New Harbinger Publications, 2011.

Hotlines, Helplines, and Online Resources

9 Tips for Finding the Right Therapist
Healthline.com/health/how-to-find-a-therapist

National Alliance on Mental Illness (NAMI)
NAMI.org
1-800-950-NAMI (6264)

National Assault Hotline (RAINN)
RAINN.org
1-866-656-HOPE (4673); TTY: 1-800-799-4889

National Suicide Prevention Lifeline
SuicidePreventionLifeline.org
1-800-273-TALK (8255)

Stop Bullying
StopBullying.gov

Substance Abuse and Mental Health Services Administration (SAMHSA)
SAMHSA.gov/find-help/national-helpline
1-800-662-HELP (4357); TTY: 1-800-487-4889

TEEN LINE

TEENLINEonline.org

1-800-TLC-TEEN (852-8336) or text "TEEN" to 83986

Youth Engaged 4 Change

Engage.youth.gov

Meditation Apps

Always remember to check with your parent or caregiver before purchasing app services.

Calm

Calm.com

My Life: Stop. Breathe. Think.

My.Life

REFERENCES

Carmody, James., and Ruth A. Baer. "Relationships between Mindfulness Practice and Levels of Mindfulness, Medical and Psychological Symptoms and Well-Being in a Mindfulness-Based Stress Reduction Program." *Journal of Behavioral Medicine* 31 (March 2008): 23–33. doi.org/10.1007/s10865-007-9130-7.

Greeson, Jeffrey M., and Gabrielle R. Chin. "Mindfulness and Physical Disease: A Concise Review." *Current Opinion in Psychology* 28 (August 2019): 204–10. doi.org/10.1016/j.copsyc.2018.12.014.

Jazaieri, Hooria, Kelly McGonigal, Thupten Jinpa, et al. "A Randomized Controlled Trial of Compassion Cultivation Training: Effects on Mindfulness, Affect, and Emotion Regulation." *Motivation and Emotion* 38 (2014): 23–35. doi.org/10.1007/s11031-013-9368-z.

McGill, Bryant, and Jenni Young McGill. *Simple Reminders: Inspiration for Living Your Best Life.* Austin, TX: Simple Reminders Publishing, LLC, 2018.

Ong, Jason, and David Sholtes. "A Mindfulness-Based Approach to the Treatment of Insomnia." *Journal of Clinical Psychology* 66, no. 11 (November 2010): 1175–84. doi.org/10.1002/jclp.20736.

Salzberg, Sharon. *Real Happiness: A 28-Day Program to Realize the Power of Meditation. 2nd ed.* New York: Workman Publishing Company, 2019.

Willard, Christopher. "Mindfulness with Youth: Sowing the Seeds of a Mindful Society." In *The Wiley Blackwell Handbook of Mindfulness*, edited by Amanda Ie, Christelle T. Ngnoumen, and Ellen J. Langer, 1071–84. New York: John Wiley & Sons, 2014.

Zoogman, Sarah, Simon B. Goldberg, William T. Hoyt, and Lisa Miller. "Mindfulness Interventions with Youth: A Meta-Analysis." *Mindfulness* 6 (2015): 290–302. doi.org/10.1007/s12671-013-0260-4.

ACKNOWLEDGMENTS

Thanks to those who have been a part of my meditation journey from my teen years onwards, especially the late Reverend Elma Lumsden of Jamaica.

Much gratitude to my parents, Alton and Carol Finnis, who have been my rock and my foundation.

Much appreciation to my encouraging prayer and meditation warriors, Bryan, Steve and Kim, Rene, Cie, Millie, Eugenia, Heidi, Angela, Mikaela, Kate, and Ms. Joan.

A big thank-you to Callisto Media for making this possible.

Special recognition goes to my young clients, whose tenacity and awesomeness continue to inspire me.

Immense thanks to my wonderful and supportive daughter, Natalia. I love you.

ABOUT THE AUTHOR

SIMONE FINNIS, LMFT, is a licensed therapist specializing in individual adult, adolescent, family, and marriage therapy. She is the founder and clinical director of Simple Therapy Now, a private practice in South Florida. She received her master's degree in marriage and family therapy from Nova Southeastern University. She is a parent educator, and the author of *If You Understood My Feelings*, and she has extensive experience working with adolescents and their families addressing a wide range of behavioral and mental health issues. Simone helps her clients discover and embrace the unique strengths and talents within them, facilitating their journey to mental and emotional well-being. In her free time, Simone enjoys the outdoors and spending time with family and friends.